LIFE SCIENCE

Protecting the Planet

KATE BOEHM JEROME

PICTURE CREDITS
Cover: © Mark Edwards/Still Pictures/Peter Arnold, Inc. Page 1 Kevin Schafer/
gettyimages; pages 2–3 Peter Timmermans/gettyimages; page 4 Todd Gipstein/
NGS Image Collection; page 5 courtesy Earth Day Canada www.earthday.ca;
page 6 from the IMAX film *Destiny in Space*, © MCMXCIV Smithsonian Institution/
Lockheed Martin Corporation ; page 7 NASA; pages 8, 9 (low right), page 11
(bottom left), 12 (top right), page 13 (right), 21 PhotoDisc®; pages 8–9 David
Doubilet/NGS Image Collection; page 9 (top) Equator Graphics; page 10 © Frans
Lanting/Minden Pictures; page 11 (top right) William Albert Allard/NGS Image
Collection; page 11 (bottom right) Annie Griffiths Bell/NGS Image Collection;
page 12 (top left) James P. Blair/NGS Image Collection; page 13 (top right) Pat
O'Hara/gettyimages; page 13 (bottom left) © Leo Keeler/Animals Animals;
pages 14–15 O. Louis Mazzatenta/NGS Image Collection; page 16 James
Richardson; page 17 David Young-Wolff/gettyimages; page 18 Philip Schermeister/
NGS Image Collection; page 19 David Woodfall/ gettyimages; page 20 © Myrleen
Ferguson/PhotoEdit; page 22 © Ray Pfortner/ Peter Arnold, Inc.; page 23
© Georgia Lowell/Science Source/Photo Researchers, Inc.; page 24 James A.
Sugar/NGS Image Collection; page 25 © Edward Parker/ Still Pictures/Peter
Arnold, Inc.; page 26 (top) © G. MacLean/OSF/Animals Animals; page 26 (mid)
© Bettmann/CORBIS; pages 28–29 Lloyd Wolf; page 29 (far right) Brian
Hagiwara/gettyimages; page 30 ©Jeff Greenberg/Peter Arnold, Inc.

Neither the publisher nor the author shall be liable for any damage that may be
caused or sustained or result from conducting any of the activities in this book
without specifically following instructions, undertaking the activities without
proper supervision, or failing to comply with the cautions contained in the book.

Produced through the worldwide resources of the National Geographic Society,
John M. Fahey, Jr., President and Chief Executive Officer; Gilbert M. Grosvenor,
Chairman of the Board; Nina D. Hoffman, Executive Vice President and
President, Books and Education Publishing Group.

PREPARED BY NATIONAL GEOGRAPHIC SCHOOL PUBLISHING
Ericka Markman, Senior Vice President and President Children's Books and
Education Publishing Group; Steve Mico, Vice President, Editorial Director;
Barbara Seeber, Editorial Manager; Lynda McMurray, Amy Sarver, Anita
Schwartz, Project Editors; Roger B. Hirschland, Consulting Editor; Jim Hiscott,
Design Manager; Karen Thompson, Art Director; Kristin Hanneman, Illustrations
Manager; Diana Bourdrez, Tom DiGiovanni, Ruth Goldberg, Stephanie Henke,
Diana Leskovac, Anne Whittle, Photo Editors; Christine Higgins, Photo Coordinator;
Matt Wascavage, Manager of Publishing Services; Sean Philpotts, Production
Manager; Jane Ponton, Production Artist.

MANUFACTURING AND QUALITY MANAGEMENT
Christopher A. Liedel, Chief Financial Officer; Phillip L. Schlosser, Director;
Clifton M. Brown III, Manager.

CONSULTANT/REVIEWER
Rebecca L. Johnson, Biologist/Science Writer, Sioux Falls, South Dakota

PROGRAM DEVELOPMENT
Kate Boehm Jerome

BOOK DESIGN
3r1 Group

Published by the National Geographic Society
1145 17th Street, N.W.
Washington, D.C. 20036-4688

ISBN: 0-7922-8864-5

Third Printing July, 2004
Printed in Canada.

Cover photo: Students in tree nursery reforest Rishi Valley in India.

Contents

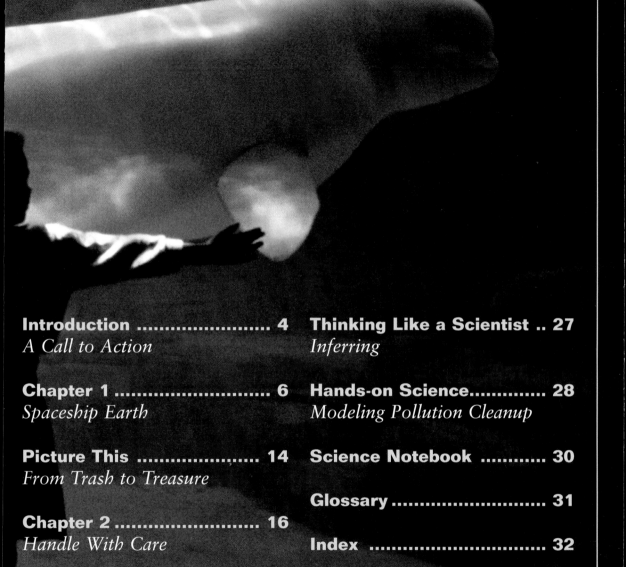

Beluga whale in the Vancouver Public Aquarium, British Columbia

A Call to Action

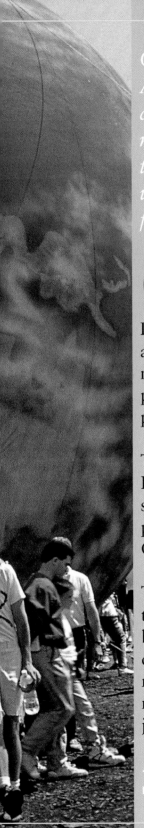

On April 22, 1970, more than 20 million Americans took part in the largest organized demonstration in history. What could draw so many people to action? Were they protesting the Vietnam War ... or staging a rally to end world hunger? No. They were demonstrating for a healthy environment.

Organizers were stunned at the number of people who participated in that first Earth Day. Since 1970 Earth Day has become an annual worldwide event. In 2001 millions of people in 184 countries took part in activities to raise awareness about pollution and other problems affecting the environment.

The success of Earth Day prompted the creation of the Environmental Protection Agency (EPA). Soon after, several important environmental protection laws were passed in the United States, including the Clean Air, Clean Water, and Endangered Species Acts.

Today most people understand that we need to protect this planet that we call home. This is a book about becoming better caretakers of Earth. We'll look at the different environments on Earth, how humans affect the resources in these environments, and how technology might shape the future. Caring for our planet is a big job—and we all need to help out.

◀ Young people—wearing T-shirts that spell out "Love your mother"—pose in front of a model of Mother Earth.

Chapter 1

Spaceship Earth

Space shuttle *Discovery*
photographed in Earth's orbit

All systems go. The astronauts blast into space. Ground control broadcasts instructions into their headsets. Check this. Report on that. When the astronauts finally get a chance to look out the window of their spacecraft, they gasp.

It's an awe-inspiring view—Earth floating as a lone planet. All of Earth's living things, including humans, exist in a region of Earth called the **biosphere**. This region extends from the deepest point in the ocean to about 8 kilometers (5 miles) into the atmosphere. The biosphere includes all the land, water, and air in which plants and animals live.

Just by looking around, you can see the many different kinds of environments in Earth's biosphere. Environments are made up of living things—plants and animals. Environments are also made up of nonliving things, such as water and air. All the living and nonliving things interacting in an area are called an **ecosystem**. A large group of similar ecosystems makes up a **biome**.

To be a good caretaker of our planet, you have to know what needs protecting. So let's explore Earth's biomes.

Diver and sweeper fish in the Red Sea

Water Biomes

Oceans cover about 70 percent of Earth's surface. So can you guess what kind of biome makes up most of the biosphere? Yes, it's water. There are two major water biomes. One is ocean waters, or the **marine** biome. The other is freshwater biomes. These are lakes, streams, rivers, and ponds.

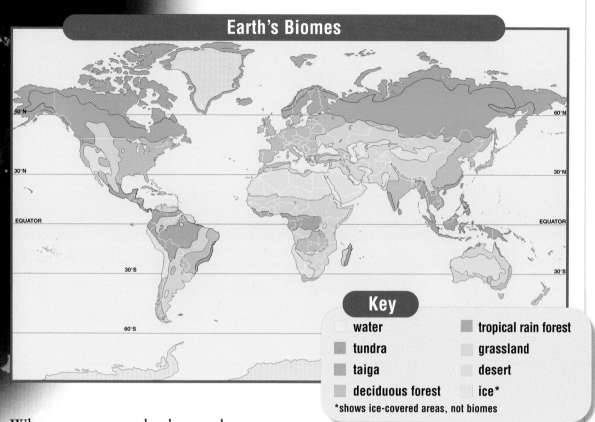

Earth's Biomes

Key

- water
- tundra
- taiga
- deciduous forest
- tropical rain forest
- grassland
- desert
- ice*

*shows ice-covered areas, not biomes

When astronauts look out the window of their spacecraft, they mostly see the marine biome. It is the largest and most widespread biome on Earth. Organisms that live in a marine biome are diverse, or different from one another. If you think about the oceans, you'll begin to see why. Shallow waters along the coast are warmed by the sun. These waters support a variety of plant and animal life. Deep ocean waters get little or no light. Temperatures can be very cold. Different types of organisms live at different depths of the ocean.

Land Biomes

The biomes we know best are the ones where we live—the land biomes. There are six major land biomes. Each has its own kind of climate, soil, plants, and animals. As you can see from the map, these six land biomes are found all over the world.

Scarlet macaw in a rain forest in Peru

The Tropical Rain Forest Biome

Tropical rain forest biomes lie close to the Equator. They have a hot and humid climate. Rainfall is frequent and heavy. Tropical rain forest biomes have about as many species of plants and animals as all the other land biomes combined.

The high trees in a rain forest biome form a dense, umbrella-like canopy. This canopy can be as high as 45 meters (148 feet) above the ground. It is so thick that little sunlight can reach the forest floor. In a rain forest biome many plants and animals live high up in the trees.

The Desert Biome

What makes a **desert**? The simple answer is very little rainfall. Organisms that live in a desert often have traits that help them conserve, or use less, water.

Most deserts are hot, partly sandy regions with few plants and animals. Earth's largest desert biome is the Sahara. It is on the continent of Africa. But did you know that not all deserts are hot? Interior lands of Antarctica (land surrounding the South Pole) receive as little **precipitation** as the Sahara. These polar deserts are extremely cold and covered in snow and ice.

The Grassland Biome

There are two types of **grassland** biomes. The **temperate** grassland usually has hot summers and cold, windy winters. The **savanna** grassland is tropical. It is usually warm all year round. Grasslands have wet and dry seasons rather than a steady flow of rain all year. They often have droughts—long periods of time when little rain falls.

Grassland in Wyoming

Along with grasses, small bushes and shrubs provide food to countless grazing animals in a grassland biome. You might wonder why many trees don't grow in a grassland biome. Long dry spells, grazing animals, and occasional fires make it hard for trees to grow and forests to form.

Desert region in Jordan

Deciduous forest in Great Smoky Mountains National Park, North Carolina

The Deciduous Forest Biome

The oak, maple, and hickory leaves in a **deciduous forest** turn blazing colors in the fall. When the leaves fall from the trees, they provide habitats for insects and spiders on the forest floor. A wide variety of animals—from skunks to snakes—also make their homes in this biome. Deciduous forests usually have warm summers. Winters are colder with frequent precipitation.

Deciduous forest biomes once covered almost all of the eastern United States and Western Europe. But many forests have been cleared away to make room for farms, cities, and towns.

The Taiga Biome

Chances are good that the paper in this book comes from trees grown in a **taiga** biome. Most paper produced in the United States and Canada is made from conifers. In a taiga forest, most of the trees are conifers like spruce and pines. Unlike deciduous trees, most conifers are evergreen. This means they keep needlelike green leaves all year long.

Taiga winters are long and cold. Summers are short and usually mild. Large animals like moose and elk share this biome with smaller ones like rabbits and owls.

The Tundra Biome

The **tundra** is cold. In fact, much of the soil in the tundra stays frozen. Winters are long and cold. Summers are short and mild. Precipitation is sparse in the tundra of the far north. In summer shallow ponds dot the landscape. They serve as breeding grounds for millions of insects, such as mosquitoes.

Caribou feed on the short grasses and low shrubs that grow in the thin layer of unfrozen soil in the tundra. Large herds migrate over long distances to find food and to keep ahead of very cold temperatures.

What other plants and animals might live in each biome?

Taiga in Olympic National Park, Washington

Tundra in Denali National Park, Alaska

Wheeled coconut-shell boat (Indonesia)

From Trash to Treasure

A simple way to protect Planet Earth is to reduce the amount of trash we throw away. Just what's in our trash? There's paper, plastics, glass, metals, and other kinds of waste. How much of that trash can be reused? How much can be turned into something useful?

Kids around the world have found some clever ways to reuse trash. They've turned their trash into toys.

Oil tanker made of pesticide cans (Senegal)

Soccer ball made of twine and plastic (Kenya)

Sardine-can pull toy (Dominica)

Gymnast made from wood and bamboo (Indonesia)

Dolls made with scraps of materials (Guatemala and Kenya)

Sailboat made of broken rubber sandal and a piece of a plastic bag (Kenya)

15

Chapter 2

Handle With Care

Save energy! Don't litter! Reduce air pollution! Keep our waterways clean! Bumper stickers and environmental slogans crop up everywhere. But do they make a difference in protecting the environment?

The answer is yes. Even the efforts of one person can help protect our planet. The issues may be easier to understand if you know not only *what* you should do but also *why* you should do it.

Consider the basics. Plants and animals, including humans, need food and water to survive. These needs are met by the natural resources found in the biosphere of Earth. To protect these resources, we need to keep the air clean and the water drinkable. We need to keep the soil healthy. How do we do that?

Protect the Land

The soil that covers fields and farms provides much of the food we eat. Human activities such as plowing fields, mining, and building highways can destroy the land. **Erosion** occurs when wind and water wear away the soil. Soil erosion and overgrazing by animals eventually can turn rich farmland into a desert wasteland. So does this mean we shouldn't build a highway or plow a field? Of course not. But it does mean we might consider Earth-friendly ways of doing those things.

Today farmers plow their fields in a variety of ways designed to prevent erosion. They try to limit the amount of water they use for their crops. They keep animals from grazing in just one area. Farmers also plant trees to prevent soil from blowing or washing away.

◄ **A girl touches the waters of Lake Itasca in Minnesota. Here the Mississippi River begins as a clear stream.**

Giant sequoia tree

Trees absorb and use carbon dioxide when they make food. Increased deforestation means fewer trees. This adds to the buildup of carbon dioxide in the air and contributes to the **greenhouse effect**. As certain gases in Earth's atmosphere increase, Earth may get too warm.

Environmentalists encourage careful management of the forests. They call for replanting after forests are cut down. They support creation of national parks to protect the forests and the animals that live there. Shortly before Earth Day 2000, President Bill Clinton dedicated a new national monument—a hiking trail through the giant sequoia trees in Sequoia National Forest in California. The President talked about John Muir, one of the country's first conservationists. He praised Muir for teaching the importance of protecting the environment more than a century ago.

Save the Trees

Another human activity that damages the land is **deforestation.** This is the removal of large numbers of trees from a forest. Millions of acres of the tropical rain forest biome are cleared away each year. When this happens, many plants and animals lose their habitat. They may die out, or become extinct. Scientists haven't even discovered all the organisms living in the tropical rain forest. We may be losing species without even knowing they exist.

Recycle, Reuse, Reduce

You wad up a piece of paper, take aim, and toss the paper into the wastebasket. It doesn't seem terribly wasteful—but it adds up. The average American produces about 10 tons of trash in 13 years.

Where does that trash go next? Much of our trash ends up in **landfills**. They take up valuable land and sometimes pollute the water, air, and land around them. More than a third of the trash in landfills is paper. Recycling, reusing, and reducing what you throw away can cut down on the need for more landfills. In fact, about 80 percent of household trash can be recycled.

Wastes from industries such as mining, manufacturing, and agriculture also cause problems. These wastes are especially harmful if they are hazardous, or dangerous, to humans and other species. The United States has passed laws to control both the disposal and the storage of hazardous wastes that may be poisonous or cause disease.

Every Drop Counts

Think of all the ways we use water. Water power supplies electricity for some homes and businesses. We drink water and wash with it. Farmers use water to irrigate their land. Much of the food we eat is either grown *with* it or caught *from* it. We use water for recreation. Clean water is essential to our lives.

But water sometimes becomes polluted. Brush your teeth or flush the toilet. The water you used isn't clean any more. In some places polluted water is released directly back into streams and lakes. This allows the growth of certain harmful bacteria, which can cause disease.

We tackle this problem in several ways. We send polluted water to water treatment plants before releasing it back into the environment. We are trying to use less water in our cities, homes, and businesses and on our farms. If we use water sparingly, there is less polluted water to clean up.

Protect the Water Supply

Surprisingly, one of the biggest sources of water pollution is the erosion of land. Sediment, or particles of soil, washing into streams and oceans can kill organisms. So by preserving plants that grow naturally, we can prevent soil erosion and also protect the water.

Toxic chemicals also threaten our water supply. Sometimes fertilizers wash off the land. They end up in the rivers, lakes, streams, and **groundwater**. Groundwater in springs and wells is the main source of drinking water for many people. Chemicals in the fertilizers that kill weeds and insects also can kill fish. They also pollute drinking water. Some poisons remain in the sediment for many years.

Action is being taken, however, to protect our water supply. Farmers are using less fertilizer or fertilizing their crops less often. Industries are being forced to pay large fines when they pollute. Some have reduced their output of hazardous waste and made other improvements to comply with the Clean Water Act.

What can you do to conserve, or use less, water every day?

Farmers use sprinklers to irrigate their fields.

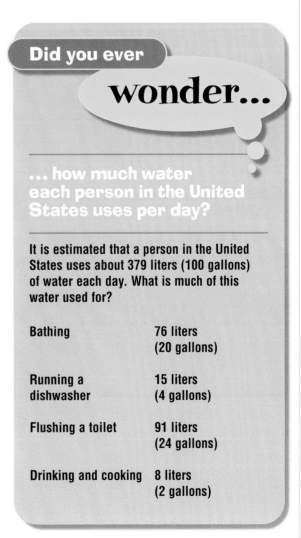

Did you ever

wonder...

... how much water each person in the United States uses per day?

It is estimated that a person in the United States uses about 379 liters (100 gallons) of water each day. What is much of this water used for?

Bathing	76 liters (20 gallons)
Running a dishwasher	15 liters (4 gallons)
Flushing a toilet	91 liters (24 gallons)
Drinking and cooking	8 liters (2 gallons)

Reduce Air Pollution

The main source of air pollution is the burning of fossil fuels. Fossil fuels, including oil, coal, and natural gas, are our main sources of energy. When energy sources are burned, sulfur and nitrogen compounds are produced. When these gases mix with moisture, they form sulfuric acid and nitric acid.

Sulfuric and nitric acids in rainwater and snow fall to Earth as acid rain. When **acid rain** falls into rivers and lakes, many organisms in these habitats cannot survive. Acid rain damages forests and crops. It also eats away at buildings, bridges, and statues.

Cars and trucks cause almost a third of the air pollution in the United States. So walking, biking, and using public transportation are ways to reduce the amount of air pollution. The buildup of pollution also comes from power plants and other industrial sources, particularly in cities in the eastern United States. To combat the problem, industries can use pollution-control devices called scrubbers on their smokestacks.

Thinking Like a Scientist: Inferring

Scientists **infer** when they make observations and use their past experiences to draw conclusions. Look carefully at this statue. It stands outside in a cemetery. When first carved, the statue was smooth and white. Now it's being worn away. Based on what you just read about air pollution, what might you infer would be one cause of the damage?

Turning to Technology

In their search for new sources of energy to protect Earth's limited resources, scientists have looked to the sun. Solar cells convert sunlight into electricity. In the future, you may be driving a car or going to a school powered by solar cells.

Solar panels reflect on a 20-story tower to create energy in California.

Technology often gets a bad rap for damaging the environment. From huge factories to little aerosol spray cans, it seems that almost every advance has taken its toll on Earth. Now may be the time when technology comes to the rescue.

New and Improved Vehicles

More than 2,000 electric-powered vehicles already travel the roads in California. Fuel-cell powered cars are another hope for the future.

Scientists developing fuel cells have been working to convert water into electricity. A device called a fuel processor separates water into its oxygen and hydrogen atoms. Then a device called a fuel cell recombines the hydrogen and oxygen to make electricity to power the car. The good news is that these energy-efficient vehicles are pollution-free. They give off only water and heat as waste. In California a Fuel Cell Partnership organization sponsored by the state has a goal of producing more than 70 fuel-cell powered vehicles by 2003.

This two-seater electric car can go 85 kilometers (53 miles) before recharging.

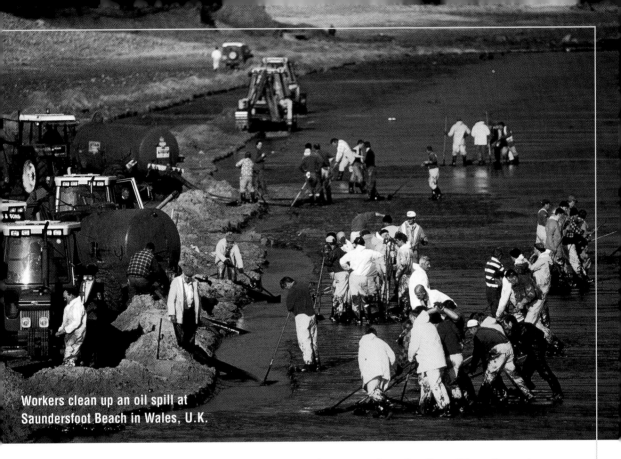

Workers clean up an oil spill at Saundersfoot Beach in Wales, U.K.

Other newly developed cars use a combination of gasoline and electricity for power. The engines in these cars have a small electric motor that reduces the amount of gas burned.

Changing Organisms

Oil companies and the government are working hard to make sure that disasters such as the 1989 *Exxon Valdez* oil spill never happen again. (The 10-million-gallon spill into Alaska's Prince William Sound was the largest in U.S. history.) There are still thousands of oil spills of various sizes, from boats, cars, and factories, reported in the U.S. each year. Just one gallon of oil can pollute up to one million gallons of water.

Bioengineering, or genetically changing an organism, may help solve this problem. Some bacteria that normally exist in the soil and water help break down oil. With new technology, scientists can bioengineer these one-celled organisms to break down oil spills faster than the naturally occurring bacteria can.

Zebrafish in Belém, Brazil

Scientists also can bioengineer larger organisms such as zebrafish to detect certain toxic chemicals in the water. An altered fish displays a certain color or glows when it encounters a pollutant. This alerts scientists to a problem.

As you can see, humans affect the biosphere in many different ways. We all need to consider our actions and their effect on Earth's natural riches. To protect our planet in the future, we must make responsible decisions today.

David Suzuki: Environmentalist

Canadian author and broadcaster David Suzuki has spent decades studying the environment. In a weekly newspaper column, "Science Matters," Suzuki asks tough questions and discusses important issues about our biosphere. He also hosts a well-known Canadian television show called *The Nature of Things*. Suzuki explains—in a way everyone can understand—how science and technology affect our lives and the world around us. On his website (*www.davidsuzuki.org*), Suzuki offers thoughtful, practical advice on how everyone can make a difference now.

Inferring

You know that observations are important in science. But sometimes we are not able to observe an event directly. When this happens, we can make an inference. Inferences are based on observations. Inferences also require us to make evaluations and draw conclusions from our own experiences.

Every year environmental groups sponsor "Beach Sweeps." These are days when volunteers pick up trash along waterfronts. One student participated in this cleanup effort and kept track of the kinds of trash she found in the two areas she cleaned. The chart below shows her findings.

Practice the Skill

Answer the following questions based on the data in the chart.
1. Which beach area has the bigger problem with trash?
2. Based on your experience, what can you infer about why one beach area is more polluted than the other?

Check It Out

In recent years several communities have been forced to close their beaches for health reasons. What might be some of the causes of these closings? How is the EPA working with state and local governments to protect beach resources?

Area 1 Beach area with restaurant		Area 2 Beach area with playground	
Item	Number Found	Item	Number Found
cigarette butt	123	cigarette butt	10
plastic bottle	8	plastic bottle	8
can	10	can	4
paper garbage	8	paper garbage	4
food garbage	5	food garbage	5

Modeling Pollution Cleanup

Water treatment plants help keep our water supply clean. In this activity you can make a model of how a filter removes some pollutants from water.

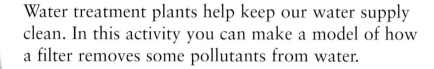

1. Make "polluted water" by mixing two tablespoons of potting soil in one-half cup of water.

2. Place the coffee filter in the funnel and put the funnel in the empty cup.

3. Pour the polluted water into the funnel. Observe what happens. (See Photograph A, below.)

4. Empty the water from the cup with the funnel.

A

B

5. Mix another two tablespoons of potting soil in one-half cup of water.

6. Now add one drop of red food coloring to the mixture and stir. (See Photograph B, above.) The food coloring represents a chemical pollutant.

7. Pour the mixture through the coffee filter and funnel.

8. Observe what happens. Compare the color of the water before and after it was filtered the second time.

Think

Did the filter remove all of the pollutants? Why do you think chemicals like chlorine have to be added to our water supply even after it has been filtered?

Science Notebook

PROGRESS REPORT

Although there is much work still to be done, the Environmental Protection Agency (EPA) reports that progress has been made in cleaning up the air and water in the United States.

- EPA's 2000 report concludes that air quality in the U.S. has continued to improve since EPA's formation in 1970. During the same time period, however, miles traveled by vehicles increased 143 percent and energy use increased by 45 percent.

- As a result of the Clean Water Act that was passed in the United States in 1972, the number of waterways that are safe for swimming and fishing has doubled.

BOOKS TO READ

Sussman, Art. *Dr. Art's Guide to Planet Earth: For Earthlings Ages 12 to 120.* Chelsea Green Publishing Co., 2000. See how systems on our planet are all connected.

Johnson, Rebecca L. *A Walk in the Desert.* Carolrhoda Books, 2000. This is one of a series of 48-page books taking the reader on a tour of the biomes of North America.

WEBSITES TO VISIT

Learn more at these websites for kids about what you can do to protect the air, water, and land.

http://www.epa.gov/kids/

http://www.kidsface.org/

http://www.worldwildlife.org/

Find out more about six of the world's major biomes.
http://mbgnet.mobot.org/sets/index.htm

Surfers protest toxic chemicals dumped in the ocean.

Glossary

acid rain – air pollution that forms when acids in the air mix with water and fall to Earth as rain or snow

bioengineering – changing the genetic makeup of an organism

biome *(BY-ohm)* – a large group of similar ecosystems

biosphere – the region in which all living things on Earth exist

deciduous *(di-SIH-joo-uhs)* **forest** – land biome with warm summers and cold winters with frequent rainfall; dominated by trees that lose their leaves each year

deforestation – the removal of large numbers of trees from a forest

desert – a land biome with very little rainfall

ecosystem – all the living and nonliving things interacting in an area

erosion – the wearing away of the land by wind and water

grassland – a land biome dominated by grasses and small bushes

greenhouse effect – the warming up of Earth's atmosphere due to the buildup of certain gases in the air

groundwater – water trapped in rocks and holes beneath Earth's surface

infer – draw conclusions based on observations and experiences

landfill – a place where garbage is dumped and covered with soil

marine – relating to the sea

precipitation – *(pri-sip-uh-TAY-shuhn)* the rain, snow, sleet, and hail that fall on Earth

savanna *(suh-VA-nuh)* – a type of grassland biome that is usually warm all year with wet and dry seasons rather than a steady flow of rain all year

taiga *(TYE-guh)* – a land biome with long, cold winters and mild summers; dominated by coniferous trees

temperate grassland – a type of grassland biome that has hot summers and cold, windy winters

tropical rain forest – a land biome with hot temperatures, frequent rainfall, and many plant and animal species

tundra *(TUHN-druh)* – a land biome with long, cold winters and short, mild summers with little rainfall and a permanently frozen layer of soil

Index